First World War
and Army of Occupation
War Diary
France, Belgium and Germany

27 DIVISION
Divisional Troops
1/1 Wessex Field Company Royal Engineers
21 December 1914 - 31 December 1915

WO95/2258/2

The Naval & Military Press Ltd
www.nmarchive.com
Published in association with The National Archives

Published by

The Naval & Military Press Ltd

Unit 10 Ridgewood Industrial Park,

Uckfield, East Sussex,

TN22 5QE England

Tel: +44 (0) 1825 749494

www.naval-military-press.com

www.nmarchive.com

This diary has been reprinted in facsimile from the original. Any imperfections are inevitably reproduced and the quality may fall short of modern type and cartographic standards.

© **Crown Copyright**
Images reproduced by permission of The National Archives, London, England, 2015.

Contents

Document type	Place/Title	Date From	Date To
Heading	WO95/2258-2		
Heading	1/1st Wessex Fld Coy R.E. Dec 1914-Dec 1915		
Heading	1st Wessex Field Coy. RE Vol I. 21.12.14-27.3.15		
Heading	War Diary of 1st Wessex Field Company R.E. From December 21st 1914 to May 31st 1915		
War Diary	Winchester	21/12/1914	22/12/1914
War Diary	Havre	23/12/1914	24/12/1914
War Diary	Blaringham	25/12/1914	05/01/1915
War Diary	Meteren	06/01/1915	07/01/1915
War Diary	Sharpensbergbeek Farm	08/01/1915	31/01/1915
War Diary	Dickebusch	08/02/1915	08/02/1915
War Diary	Reninghelst	09/02/1915	16/02/1915
War Diary	Dickebusch	22/02/1915	01/03/1915
War Diary	Reninghelst	07/03/1915	03/04/1915
War Diary	Ypres	04/04/1915	08/04/1915
War Diary	Potijze	11/04/1915	02/05/1915
War Diary	Brandhoek	03/05/1915	08/05/1915
War Diary	Ypres	09/05/1915	31/05/1915
Heading	1st Wessex Field Coy RE Vol II 1-30.6.15		
Heading	War Diary 1st Wessex Fd Coy RE June 1915		
War Diary		01/06/1915	01/06/1915
War Diary	Erquinghem	02/06/1915	30/06/1915
Heading	War Diary Of 1st Wessex Field Company R.E. From July 1st 1915 To July 31st 1915 Vol III		
War Diary	Erquinghem	01/07/1915	31/07/1915
Heading	War Diary Of 1st Wessex Field Company Royal Engineers 27th Division From 1st August 1915 To 31st Oct 1915 Vol IV		
War Diary Diagram etc	Erquinghem	01/08/1915	03/08/1915
War Diary	Erquinghem	04/08/1915	15/09/1915
War Diary	Bleutour	16/09/1915	19/09/1915
War Diary	Thiennes	20/09/1915	20/09/1915
War Diary	Mericourt	21/09/1915	30/09/1915
War Diary	Mericourt-S-Somme	01/10/1915	09/10/1915
War Diary	Chuignolles	10/10/1915	18/10/1915
War Diary	Mericourt	19/10/1915	24/10/1915
War Diary	Boves	25/10/1915	25/10/1915
War Diary	Seux	26/10/1915	26/10/1915
War Diary	Hermilly	27/10/1915	31/10/1915
Heading	War Diary Of 1st Wessex Field Company RE (T.F.) (27th Division) Vol V		
War Diary	Hermilly	01/11/1915	22/11/1915
War Diary	Saisseval	23/11/1915	30/11/1915
Heading	War Diary Of 1st Wessex Field Coy R.E. (T.F.)-27th Div. From 1st Dec 1915 To 31st Dec 1915 Vol. VI		
War Diary	Saisseval	01/12/1915	06/12/1915
War Diary	Clairy	07/12/1915	09/12/1915
War Diary	Marseilles	10/12/1915	13/12/1915
War Diary	Borely Parc Marseilles	14/12/1915	31/12/1915

War Diary   Xmas Day

west / 2258(2)

west / 2258(2)

27TH DIVISION
DIVL ENGINEERS

1/1ST WESSEX FLD COY R.E.
DEC 1914 — DEC 1915

NUMBERED 500 from 1 to 7

24th Division

1st Sussex Field Coy: RE.

Vol I. 21.12.14 —— 31.5.15

21.12.14 — 27.5.15

12/5/25

Confidential.

War Diary

of

1ˢᵗ Wessex Field Company R.E.

From December 21ˢᵗ 1914 — To May 31ˢᵗ 1915

1st WESSEX FIELD Cº R.E. (T.)

Army Form C. 2118.

WAR DIARY
or
INTELLIGENCE SUMMARY.
(Erase heading not required.)

Instructions regarding War Diaries and Intelligence Summaries are contained in F.S. Regs., Part II. and the Staff Manual respectively. Title pages will be prepared in manuscript.

Hour, Date, Place		Summary of Events and Information	Remarks and references to Appendices
1914			
December 21st	WINCHESTER	Leave camp 8am – march to SOUTHAMPTON and embark on the CHYBASSA at 5 P.m.	
" 22nd	—	—	
" 23rd	— HAVRE	Land at HAVRE. 3 P.m. Leave docks complete at 12 midnight and march to Camp d'Oisene.	
" 24th	—	Leave this Camp at 4.30 P.m. and entrain by 7.30 – Train leaves at 11.20 – first stop ROUEN	
"	—	Travelling all day – reach ARQUES about 9 P.m. & detrain. Ready to march about 12 midnight –	
" 25th	BLARINGHAM	Reach Billets at Blaringham about 6am	
" 27th	"	Start work on line of Trenches –	
" 28th	"	Working at Trenches and instructing the infantry units.	
" 29th	"	do	
" 30th	"	do	
" 31st	"	do	
1915 –			
January 1st	"	Inspection by Gen¹ Trench in line of Trenches –	
" 2nd	"	huge Sutton & 1 NCO. go by bus to the Trenches in front line. Have a march out at 8.30 P.m. of 2 miles way –	
" 3rd	"	Have orders to move early tomorrow –	
" 4th	"	(Subaltern at 8 tomorrow – major Sutton in...	

WAR DIARY
or
INTELLIGENCE SUMMARY.
(Erase heading not required.)

Army Form C. 2118.

Hour, Date, Place	Summary of Events and Information	Remarks and references to Appendices
1915.		
January 5th BLARINGHAM.	Leave Blaringham at 8am and march via SERCUS - HAZEBROUCK - CAESTRE - FLÊTRE to METEREN - Billeted here for the night.	
6th METEREN.	Taken over portion in Col. at 10% and march via BAILLEUL entering BELGIUM at 11.20 - Halt at LA CLYTTE and find billets - One Brigade the 80th takes over the trenches from the French same evening.	
7th	Move to new billets at SHARPENSBERGBEEK FARM - + share with officers of Ammunition Col.	
8th SHARPENSBERG--BEEK FARM	Our Sections on R.E. Works forming S.E.	
9th "	Work in front-line trenches	
10th "	Take various loads of fascines, Runners etc. to DICKEBUSCH.	
11th "	Start Bomb Proof shelters at DICKEBUSCH.	
12th "	Our sections in the trenches to-night	
13th "	1 & 2 Sections in Trenches	
14th "	" " " "	
15th "	Start shelters in wood behind DICKEBUSCH.	
16th "	Continue " " " "	
17th "	" " " "	
18th "	Heavy Snow storm - " " " "	
19th "	Continue shelters " " "	
20th "	Work on flooring and - Second line made Capt Merrice & Sankey Major	
"	Sections work on Second line trenches	

Army Form C. 2118.

WAR DIARY
or
INTELLIGENCE SUMMARY.
(*Erase heading not required.*)

Instructions regarding War Diaries and Intelligence Summaries are contained in F.S. Regs., Part II. and the Staff Manual respectively. Title pages will be prepared in manuscript.

(3)

Hour, Date, Place		Summary of Events and Information	Remarks and references to Appendices
January	1915		
	21st	Known R.E. Work. 2½ line Trenches – Huts & Roads 4th	
	22nd	"	
	23rd	"	
	24th	"	
	25th	"	
	26th	"	
	27th	"	
	28th	"	
	29th	"	
	30th	"	
	31st	Move to DICKEBUSCH	
February			
DICKEBUSCH	8th	Start at 9 a.m. for weeks rest at PENINGHELST	
PENINGHELST	9th	Major Dutton leaves us on leave	
"	14th	R. Carr who was with our Co was killed at S⁺ ELOI	
"	15th	Return to DICKEBUSCH – Billeted in huts	
DICKEBUSCH	21st	Major Dutton returns	
March			
"	1st	Move back to PENINGHELST for next week – L⁺ Blac arrives from Reserve Bn – Captain Jones leaves us for CRE's Office as acting Adjutant	

Army Form C. 2118.

WAR DIARY
or
INTELLIGENCE SUMMARY.
(Erase heading not required.)

(4)

Hour, Date, Place	Summary of Events and Information	Remarks and references to Appendices
1915		
March 7. RENINGHELST	Start back to DICKEBUSCH - h Back at this time -	
13 "	Major Dutton goes to Hospital.	
14 "	Company stand to all night - while the attack at St ELOI is on -	
16 "	Lieut Godsell of the 177 Co R.E. attached to us -	
19 "	Show Officers from the Cheshire R.E's over the Trenches & hand same over.	
23 "	Return to RENINGHELST at 1 p.m. Have first man killed at 12 a.m in morning in Trenches	
24 "	Sections all at work on GHQ Line & Trenches - DICKEBUSCH during night	
26 "	C.R.E, inspects the Company - "Harvey Brown joins us from Reserve Company	
27 "	Head Officer to YPRES to inspect & report on Trenches there.	

Army Form C. 2118.

WAR DIARY
or
INTELLIGENCE SUMMARY.
(Erase heading not required.)

1 Sept 7 Coy RE

Place	Date	Hour	Summary of Events and Information	Remarks and references to Appendices
RENINGHELST	April 2		Major Dearsley R.E. takes over command of the Company.	
	3		O.C. inspects the Company	
	YPRES 4		Company move to YPRES at 4.50 P.M. — Billet.	
	5		Two Sections (1+3) go to front-line trenches — live in Dugouts — up for 4 days.	
	8		The Company change Billets — sharing half of a hospital with a Field Ambulance	
	POTIJZE 10		The Company move to POTIJZE — Light Casualties and minor Gas "Panic" up the line too.	
	15		Arrange Billets for mining section who are attached to us	
	16		The whole Company "stand to" all night.	
	17		Do Do	
	19	7am	Officers Billet in Office blown in by Shell. 2 O.R. Frew killed. Major Dearsley + Lieut Service slightly wounded.	

Army Form C. 2118.

WAR DIARY
or
INTELLIGENCE SUMMARY.
(Erase heading not required.)

Instructions regarding War Diaries and Intelligence Summaries are contained in F.S. Regs., Part II. and the Staff Manual respectively. Title pages will be prepared in manuscript.

Hour, Date, Place	Summary of Events and Information	Remarks and references to Appendices
April 20 POTIJZE	Hutsite heavily shelled all day. Bring up Pontoons from Busseboom for pontoon bridge over YPRES moat.	
21 "	New billets again shelled – in village of POTIJZE.	
22 "	Very heavy bombardment. Working parties at advance dugouts ordered to stand to. Feel effects of Gas for first time.	
23 "	Heavy bombardment continues – Advance working sections ordered to return to POTIJZE – Officers billet shelled. All sections at work on Dugouts – near the road – Night work on 2nd Line	
24 "	All men sleep in Dugouts. Heavy shelling continues – YPRES in flames. Working parties withdrawn from 2nd Line early in afternoon.	
25 "	Sections standing to all day.	
26. "	Our Dugouts shelled. Several men wounded, and also horses – many of them having to be shot. Major Dutton returns in evening.	
27 "	The whole Company under Majors Dutton & Sankey at work on the Switch Line. Major Dutton goes up to front line billets.	
28 "	Major Sankey leaves us.	
29 "	Many more men & horses wounded by shells	
30 "	Capt Harvey returns, and proceeds to front line. Things much quieter.	

1915

WAR DIARY
or
INTELLIGENCE SUMMARY.
(Erase heading not required.)

Army Form C. 2118.

1st Wessex Fd. Coy R.E.

Hour, Date, Place	Summary of Events and Information	Remarks and references to Appendices
May. 1. POTIJZE	A quiet day. Sections at work on supporting points & improving 2nd line.	
2. "	Gas comes over our dug-outs from firing line again. At 10.45 am the HQrs are ordered to take for a back position between POPERINGHE and VLAMERTINGHE any time after 12 mid-night – Leave at 1am & Arr. several horses missing.	
3. BRANDHOEK	Arrive at BRANDHOEK at 4am. Find billets. All sections working in front line.	
4. "	Vet inspects horses – we are 38 short.	
5. "	Capt Noble (Adjutant CRE 27 Div) inspects billets.	
6. "	Col. Walker (CRE) calls and inspects billets. 2nd Lt ??? is lent temporarily to the 2nd Wessex F.E.	
7. "	Lt. H. Brown takes over the HQrs. Lieut IN Harcourt returning to Front line at Railway Dugouts.	
8. "	Attack by enemy compels us to leave dug-outs which are blown in. 1.3.4A sections assist cavalry with guns and later take up quarters for the night in GHQ line.	

WAR DIARY
INTELLIGENCE SUMMARY
(Erase heading not required.)

Army Form C. 2118.

Hour, Date, Place	Summary of Events and Information	Remarks and references to Appendices
May 9th YPRES		
10	Sections 1 & 2 with Major & Capt return to CASEMATES in YPRES. Sections 3 & 4 remain in GHQ line. Lieut Chasey wounded by shrapnel in leg.	
11	Whole Company working on a reserve trench.	
12	Lt. S. Maurice killed in action about 2.30 am on MENIN ROAD.	
13	All Sections on night work at HOOGE. Constructing new trenches, improving communications etc.	
14	Sections 3 & 4 return to CASEMATES after work.	
15	One Section lent to the 177th Field Co. R.E.? Other Sections entrenching at HOOGE	
16	Do Do	
17	Whole Company at at work in trenches at night.	
18	Lt. Pitt returns to us.	
19	Nos 1 & 2 Sections at work on G.H.Q. Line. Nos 3 & 4 on 2nd line in SANCTUARY WOOD.	
22	Major Sandys takes Section to work for Cavalry on GHQ Line.	
23	Capt Harvey returns to England on leave	
25	All Sections back from YPRES	
26	Two Sections working each night on supporting points at Reserve	
27	Farm & in neighbourhood of MAPLE COPSE.	
28		
29	Capt Harvey returns from leave. Two sections at work on G.H.Q. Line at [illegible] crossing MENIN ROAD.	

WAR DIARY
or
INTELLIGENCE SUMMARY.
(Erase heading not required.)

Army Form C. 2118.

Hour, Date, Place	Summary of Events and Information	Remarks and references to Appendices
1915 May 30th	Sections 1, 2 & 4 Section left dug-outs near VLAMERTINGHE & joined Company at BRANDHOEK. Men refitted & spent rest of day loading wagons & preparing for tomorrows move.	
" 31st	Company left billets at BRANDHOEK at 9.30 a.m. & joined 17th Field Co. at rendezvous on VLAMERTINGHE — OUDERDOM road at 10.0 a.m. Marched via ZEVERCOTEN — LOCRE — DRANOUTRE to billets at a farm 2 miles S.W. of latter place where we spent night.	

29th Division.

1st Wessex Field Coy RE.

Vol II 1 — 30.6.15.

13/6015

a97
DJW

Confidential

War Diary,
1st Canadian F. Coy R.E.
June 1915

WAR DIARY 1st WESSEX FIELD Co. R.E. (T.)
or
INTELLIGENCE SUMMARY.
(Erase heading not required.)

Army Form C. 2118.

Instructions regarding War Diaries and Intelligence Summaries are contained in F.S. Regs., Part II. and the Staff Manual respectively. Title pages will be prepared in manuscript.

Hour, Date, Place	Summary of Events and Information	Remarks and references to Appendices
1915 June 1st	Rained 4.0 a.m. Company left billets near DRANOUTRE at 6.0 a.m. & marched via BAILLEUL and TABOT to ERQUINGHEM (LYS) where we arrived at 10.30 a.m. Sappers were comfortably arranged for in billets at school.	
ERQUINGHEM. 1915 June 2nd	No.1 Section took over work in R.E. workshops from 20th Co. R.E. Nos. 2, 3 & 4 Section cleaning up and & checking & repairing tools. No.4 Sec. at work on 2nd line at night. O.C. & Field Pk. made tour of fans of front line. Capt. Harvey reconnoitred position for two pontoon bridges on LYS.	
ERQUINGHEM 1915 June 3rd	No.1 Sec. & carpenters in R.E. workshops. No.2 Sec. repairing tools. No.3 Sec. built pontoon bridge across LYS near ARMENTIÈRES & afterwards dismantled same. No.4 Sec. at work on 2nd line at night.	
ERQUINGHEM 1915 June 4th	Nos. 1 & 2 Section same as yesterday. No.3 Sec. at work on 2nd line at night. No.4 Sec. removing explosives from billets and preparing dug-outs for same near ERQUINGHEM Bridge. O.C. & Capt. Harvey made tour of trenches occupied by 2nd Royal Welsh Fusiliers.	
ERQUINGHEM 1915 June 5th	Nos. 1 & 2 Section same as before. No.3 Sec. work on 2nd line at night & erecting M.G. emplacement in front line trenches. No.4 Sec. built pontoon bridge across LYS at BRASSERIE near BAC ST MAUR & afterwards dismantled.	
ERQUINGHEM 1915 June 6th	Company engaged in preparing material for pontoons. Church Parade at 7.30 a.m.	

WAR DIARY
of
INTELLIGENCE SUMMARY

1st WESSEX FIELD Co. R.E. (T.)

Army Form C. 2118.

(Erase heading not required.)

Hour, Date, Place	Summary of Events and Information	Remarks and references to Appendices
ERQUINGHEM 1915 June 7th	1st Parade:- Physical & recreation drill. 2nd " :- No.1 Sec. bridging L/S at BRASSERIE near BAC ST MAUR and at night on work in support line. No.2 Sec. & carpenters in R.E. workshops. No.3 Sec. drainage & revetting parapet of support line nr. DEADCOW FARM. No.4 Sec. deepening & improving PARK ROW communication trench	
ERQUINGHEM 1915 June 8th	1st Parade as yesterday. Surveying Parties:- No.2 Sec. & carpenters in workshops & hutting at CROIX DU BAC. No.3 Sec. revetting parapet & improving support trench at DEADCOW FARM. No.4 Sec. & building trench traverses & loopholes in PARK ROW. No.1 Sec. on night work on support line. Brig. Gen. Golden VC. by fire inspected Coy. at 6.0 a.m.	
ERQUINGHEM 1915 June 9th	1st Parade as before. Paras. Nos. 1, 2 & 3 Sections' name as yesterday. No.4 Section numbering & placing direction boards in front line, also communication trenches.	
ERQUINGHEM 1915 June 10th	1st Parade as before. Later, No.1 Sec. at night to support line nr BURNT FARM with civilians. No.2 Sec. & carpenters in workshops & hutting. No.3 Sec. & 4 Sec. improving defences of DEADCOW FARM & drainage of communication trench. Also strengthening any weakening party in PARK ROW.	
ERQUINGHEM 1915 June 11th	Same as yesterday.	

WAR DIARY
INTELLIGENCE SUMMARY.

1st WESSEX FIELD Co R.E. (T.)   Army Form C. 2118.

(Erase heading not required.)

Instructions regarding War Diaries and Intelligence Summaries are contained in F. S. Regs., Part II and the Staff Manual respectively. Title pages will be prepared in manuscript.

Hour, Date, Place	Summary of Events and Information	Remarks and references to Appendices
ERQUINGHEM 1915 June 12th	Sections continued same work as yesterday & also repaired road between near BOIS GRENIER	
ERQUINGHEM 1915 June 13th	Nos. 1 & 2 Sec. in workshops preparing materials for trenches. No. 3 & 4 Sec. on defences of JERICOW FARM. O.C. accompanied Lord Loppell & C.R.E. on inspection of RUE DE BOIS trenches. Capt. Harvey made reconnaissance of proposed roadway from the ARMENTIÈRES — ERQUINGHEM road through RUE FLEURIE to FARM DESPLANQUE.	
ERQUINGHEM 1915 June 15th	Nos. 1 & 4 Sect. on defences of BEACOW FARM & other works in vicinity. No. 2 Sec. at work hacking support line N. of BURNT FARM wire obstacles. No. 3 Sec. & carpenters in the workshops.	
June 16th	Nos. 1 & 4 Secs. preparing BURNT FARM defences, sandbag revetting, loopholing, &c. Nos. 2 & 3 Sec. same as yesterday.	
ERQUINGHEM 1915 June 17th	As yesterday.	

WAR DIARY

INTELLIGENCE SUMMARY

1st WESSEX FIELD Coy R.E. (T.)

Army Form C. 2118.

Hour, Date, Place	Summary of Events and Information	Remarks and references to Appendices
ERQUINGHEM. 1915 June 18th	Nos 1 & 4 Sec. on defences of BURNT FARM & revetting adjoining trenches. No. 2 Sect. at night on support line work civilians. No. 3 Sec. & carpenters at work in like workshops. 2nd Lieut. Aspland joins Coy & is posted to command No. 3 Sectn.	
ERQUINGHEM. 1915 June 19th	Lieut. Lott goes on leave to England. Sections continued work as yesterday. Capt. Harvey & 2nd Lieut. Aspland inspected new working party of 1 Coy. A. & S. Highlanders on support line as no 1.	
ERQUINGHEM 1915 June 20th	Nos. 1 & 4 Sections continued work as before. Nos. 2 & 3 Sections afternoon free. Sections prepared for Church Parade at 6.0 p.m.	
ERQUINGHEM. 1915 June 21st	No. 1 Sec. drawing & improving defences of BURNT FARM. " 2 Sec. erecting new screen Long pond between NEW FARM and 3018 GRENIER. No. 3 Sec. revetting ravine support line at night with civilians. No. 4 Sec. & Carpenters in workshop.	
ERQUINGHEM. 1915 June 22nd	Sections at work as yesterday.	

WAR DIARY
or
INTELLIGENCE SUMMARY.

1st WESSEX FIELD Co. R.E. (T.)

Army Form C. 2118.

(Erase heading not required.)

Hour, Date, Place	Summary of Events and Information	Remarks and references to Appendices
ERQUINGHEM 1915 June 23	Sections continued work as yesterday. 2/Lieut. Oxland made roll call counter/supply reconnaissance.	
June 24	Sections at work as before, including trenches in DEADCOW FARM & trench wire entanglement in support line.	
June 25	Sections continued work already begun. Capt. Harvey made bridge reconnaissance over moat at FLAMENGRIE FARM and prepared plans.	
June 26	All sections continued work as before. Lieut. Pitt returned from leave.	
June 27	Nos. 1 & 2 Sections continued work on support line, & BURNT FARM & finished erecting road screen. No. 3 & 4 Sections preparing materials in workshop except 10 o'clock afternoon free.	
June 28	No. 1 Sec. & carpenters took over work in R.E. workshops. No. 2 Sec. & dug outs on support line near STANWAY AVENUE. No. 3 Sec. ditto near BURNT FARM. No. 4 Sec. in workshop till midday and on entanglement of support line at night. Corpl. Rablett of Wl.A Section was killed outside working on support line at 11.15 p.m. Bullet in stomach.	

WAR DIARY
or
INTELLIGENCE SUMMARY.
(Erase heading not required.)

Army Form C. 2118.

1st WESSEX FIELD Co. R.E. (T.)

Hour, Date, Place	Summary of Events and Information	Remarks and references to Appendices
ERQUINGHEM. 1915 June 29	No. 1 Sec. & carpenters in workshops. No. 2 Sec. on drainage and improvement of PARK ROW communication trench. No. 3 Sec. on trenches near BURNT FARM and dug-outs in support line. No. 4 Sec. on wire entanglement of support line at night and superintending civilian filling in revetment of parapet.	
June 30.	No. 1 Sec. as yesterday. No. 2 Sec. on morning cleaning and painting tools, cart and as night with No. 4 Sec. on entanglement of support line. No. 3 Sec. on dug-outs in support line near DEADCOW FARM.	S P Rowley Capt. 1st Wessex Fd Co R.E. R.M. Dutton Major OC 1st Wx Fd Co RE

27th Division

Confidential

TITLE

War Diary

of

1st Wessex Field Company R.E.

From July 1st 1915 To July 31st 1915

Vol III

Army Form C. 2118.

WAR DIARY
or
INTELLIGENCE SUMMARY.

1st Wessex Field Co. R.E.

(Erase heading not required.)

Instructions regarding War Diaries and Intelligence Summaries are contained in F.S. Regs., Part II and the Staff Manual respectively. Title pages will be prepared in manuscript.

Hour, Date, Place	Summary of Events and Information	Remarks and references to Appendices
ERQUINGHEM 1st July 1915	No. 1 Section with carpenters in Company workshops. No. 2 Section cleaning and boarding Company wagons in preparation for moving out. No. 3 Section to wire entanglements & dug outs on support line Nos. 2 & 3 Sector in day and during the night.	
2nd July 1915	No. 1 & 3 Sections as yesterday. No. 2 Section moved from Pte to new area not far from FORT J. FROMBARRE FARM. No. 1 & 3 Sections and Eng HQ bivouac at new dugouts. Nos. 1 commenced revetted to No 2 of Strong Points reported to Brigade.	
3rd July 1915	All sections at work as yesterday. High working party from Saltfield Bolir. removed chiefly of carpenters to help maintain reported to Brigade.	
4th July 1915	Sections continued work as before & in addition surveyed small crossing pts near L'ARMEE, cleaning out, revetted & repairing. L'ARMEE de LAIES. Small parade at 10.30 am.	
5th July 1915	No. 2 Section in afternoon with carpenters. Nos. 1 & 3 Section at work with infantry working parties on new dug-outs for A and B Coys. the 1/4 Rifles & BURNT FARM dug-outs. Cleaning out at FORT No. 7. Existing links near L'ARMEE.	
6th July 1915	All Sections at work as yesterday. Also Sub/Lt commissioning firing worked with Lieutenants from picked supports in FORT FREVIER.	

(73989) W4141—463. 400,000. 9/14. H.&J.Ltd. Forms/C. 2118/10.

Army Form C. 2118.

WAR DIARY
or
INTELLIGENCE SUMMARY.
(Erase heading not required.)

1st Wessex Field Co. R.E.

Instructions regarding War Diaries and Intelligence Summaries are contained in F. S. Regs., Part II. and the Staff Manual respectively. Title pages will be prepared in manuscript.

Hour, Date, Place	Summary of Events and Information	Remarks and references to Appendices
ERQUINGHEM 7th July 1915	No. 1 & 2 Sections erecting huts, cleaning walls, & collecting tar for use in same. Rest sections marched to Baths in afternoon. No. 2 Sect. in company workshop. No. 4 Sec. on dugouts at BURNT FARM.	
8th July 1915	No. 1 & 3 Sections preparing material in afternoon & at night with infantry working parties on new dug-out line. No. 2 Section working in Co. Sec. improving trench on right of COM LANE and repairing footbridge near VOCKS COR. No. 4 Section at Ratts.	
9th July 1915	All Sections at work as yesterday. No. 4 Section also repairing bridge across R. LAIES near LONDON BRIDGE.	
10th July 1915	Sections at work as yesterday, also repairing screen on Bois GRENIER ROAD & renewing damaged huts near STREAKY BACON.	
11th July 1915	No. 2 Section morning in workshop & at night on new dug-out line with infantry working parties. No. 4 Section improving latrines at ARGYLE St. at manuals & at night on dug-out line. Special respirator parade at 5.15 pm. Church Parade at 6.0 pm.	
12th July 1915	No. 1 Section on trench to right of ARGYLE ST. No. 3 Sec. in workshop. No. 2 & 4 Sections preparing materials in afternoon & at night with infantry working parties on dug-out line.	

Army Form C. 2118.

WAR DIARY
or
INTELLIGENCE SUMMARY.

1st Sussex Field Co. R.E.

(Erase heading not required.)

Instructions regarding War Diaries and Intelligence Summaries are contained in F.S. Regs., Part II. and the Staff Manual respectively. Title pages will be prepared in manuscript.

Hour, Date, Place	Summary of Events and Information	Remarks and references to Appendices
ERQUINGHEM 13th July 1915	All sections at work as yesterday. Bayonet scaling steel joists from ARMENTIERES.	
14th July 1915	No. 1, 3 & 4 Sections at work as yesterday. No. 2 Section cutting picks and preparing material for shoring dugouts. Lieut Rothband's Report go to Croix du Bac to attend S.L.B. Bomb throwing course.	
15th July 1915	No. 1 Section improving dugout near the hospital. No. 2 Section supplying dugouts in front of locus star. No. 3 Section working a B. in Section preparing material in afternoon & arranging paving in PRINCES ST. No. 1 & 3 Sections attend a Route.	
16th July 1915	Lost as yesterday. Bayonet with Railings joined to mmmmmmmmmm Sections continued work as before.	
17th July 1915		
18th July 1915	No 1 Section with infantry parties on the and line near LOW AVE and in PRINCES ST. No 2 Section repairing screen on LOOS GROVE Send Cpl Buck was severely wounded by bullet while sawing wood in short street. No 3 & 4 sections preparing education workshop. Special requisition parade at 4.15 pm Lieut Lewis at 6.0 pm	

(73989) W 4141—463. 400,000. 9/14. H.&J.Ltd. Forms/C. 2118/10.

Army Form C. 2118.

WAR DIARY
or
INTELLIGENCE SUMMARY.

1st Wessex Field Co. R.E.

(Erase heading not required.)

Instructions regarding War Diaries and Intelligence Summaries are contained in F.S. Regs., Part II and the Staff Manual respectively. Title pages will be prepared in manuscript.

Hour, Date, Place	Summary of Events and Information	Remarks and references to Appendices
ERQUINGHEM		
19th July 1915	Nos. 1 & 2 Sections roofing new dug-outs. No. 3 Sec. repairing screen on BOIS GRENIER Road & cutting posts for dug-out roofs. No. 4 Section in workshops.	
20th July 1915	Sections engaged as yesterday. Nos. 3 & 4 Sections attend baths.	
21st July 1915	No. 1 Section roofing dug-outs in Left Sector. No. 2 Section in Right Sector. No. 3 Section in centre Sector. No. 4 Section with carpenters & smiths in workshops.	
22nd July 1915	All Sections at work as yesterday. Lieut. Capt. Picken joins Company.	
23rd July 1915	Do.	
24th July 1915	Do. { Lieut. Capt. Picken reverts to 2nd Lieut. { Ranking of 2nd Lieut.	
25th July 1915	Do. Rifle Inspection at 5.15 p.m.	
26th July 1915	Church parade at 6.0 p.m.	
	Nos. 1 & 3 Sections jogging new dug-outs. No. 2 Section cutting steel joists and preparing material for right angles on dug-outs. No. 4 Section in workshops. Offr. parties cleaning wells, superintending civilian on drainage of R. de Paies and repairing tubs with fleet.	
27th July 1915	Work continued as yesterday.	

Army Form C. 2118.

WAR DIARY 1st Wessex Field Co. R.E.
or
INTELLIGENCE SUMMARY.
(Erase heading not required.)

Instructions regarding War Diaries and Intelligence Summaries are contained in F. S. Regs., Part II. and the Staff Manual respectively. Title pages will be prepared in manuscript.

Hour, Date, Place	Summary of Events and Information	Remarks and references to Appendices
ERQUINGHEM. 28th July 1915	Nos 1 & 3 Sections staying war diagrams. No 2 Section preparing material in afternoon & at night on dugouts, loop holes and workshop and no Company diagrams at ERQUINGHEM. No 4 Section on 1st period work.	
29th July 1915	Sections at work as yesterday. Party of sappers and sawyer starting new bespoke dugouts near LA VESEE.	
30th July 1915	Sections continued work as yesterday.	
31st July 1915	Nos 1 & 2 Sections continued work as usual & at night took Ee similar work by day on loop expected places. No 2 Section on nightly Road of sappers & sawyers on dugouts near Specified days returned to Co as no more to find Every day throughout the week the men have had instruction and physical drill in early morning & evening	R.H.Dutton Major o/c 1st Wx Fd 7p.1, R.E.

J. Rush Catton
Capt 87½
13-8-15

27th Division

CONFIDENTIAL

12/7493

WAR DIARY

of

1ST WESSEX FIELD COMPANY ROYAL ENGINEERS

27TH DIVISION

Vol VI

FROM 1ST AUGUST 1915 TO 31ST OCT 1915.

[Signed] Webb
Capt RE
Adjutant 27th Div Eng'rs
for CRE 27th Division

[Stamp: HEADQUARTERS 6 – NOV. 1915 27th DIVISIONAL ENGINEERS]

Army Form C. 2118.

WAR DIARY or INTELLIGENCE SUMMARY.

1st Wessex Field Co. R.E.

(Erase heading not required.)

Instructions regarding War Diaries and Intelligence Summaries are contained in F.S. Regs., Part II. and the Staff Manual respectively. Title pages will be prepared in manuscript.

Hour, Date, Place	Summary of Events and Information	Remarks and references to Appendices
ERQUINGHEM	No. 1 Section built and afterwards dismantled pontoon bridge at Blancherie H5-a-4-7.	
	No. 2 Section do. at Brasserie near 34C St Yvon	
	Both Sections checked stores to see that everything was in place in case of emergency.	
	No. 3 Section on dug-outs near N. Princess St. until 10 a.m.	
	10 a.m. Section in dug-outs & looking ahead for anti-gas work	
	Special parade for inspection of Respirators & Smoke Helmets at 5.0 p.m.	
	Patrol parade at 5.45 p.m. followed by Roll Call [?]	
	No. 1 Section Repairing material & wiring in the new Front Line.	
	2 Sec. at work on M.G. Emplacements [?]	
	3 Sec. [illegible]	

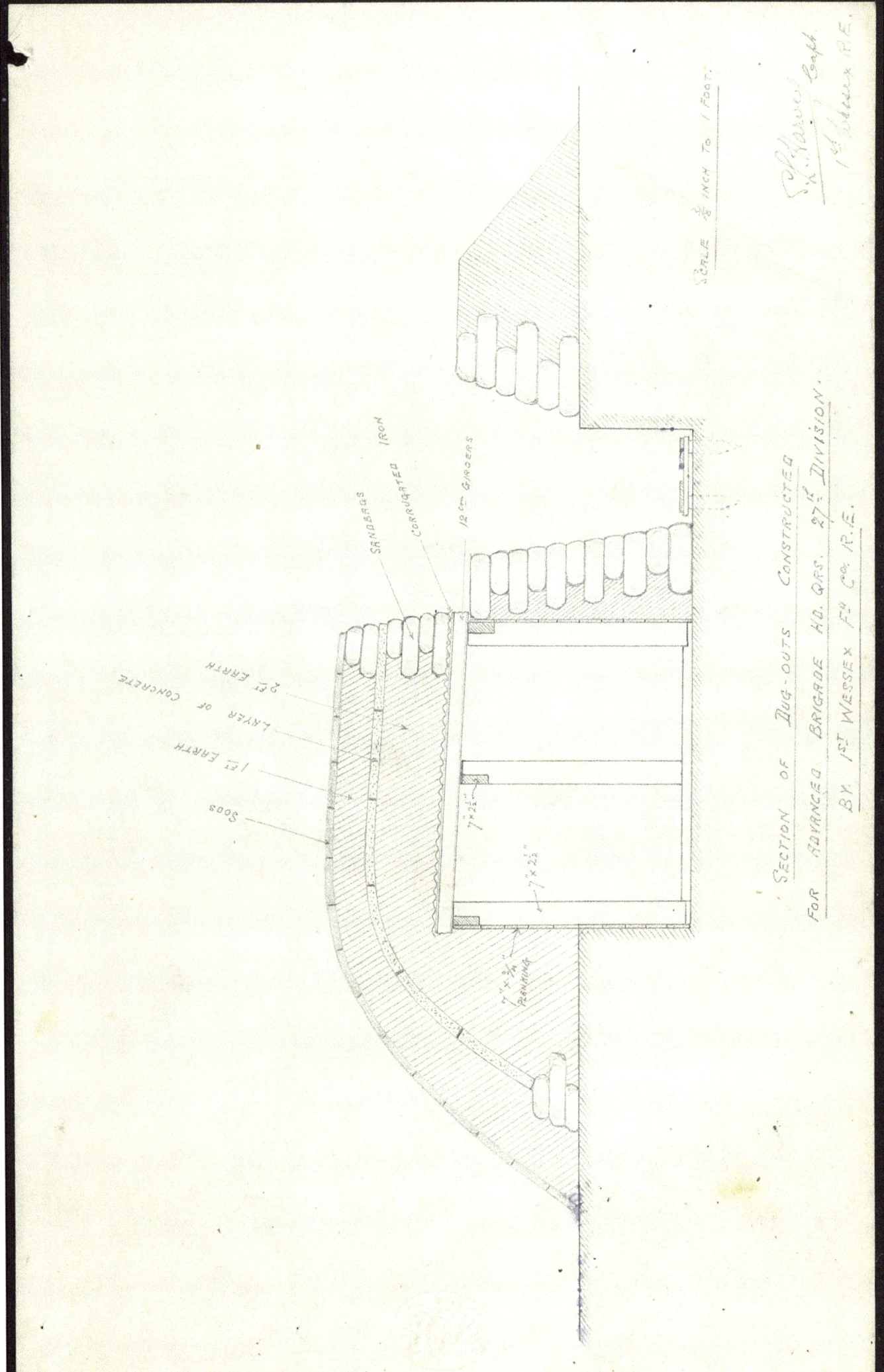

Army Form C. 2118.

WAR DIARY
or
INTELLIGENCE SUMMARY.
(Erase heading not required.)

[Essex Field Co. R.E.]

Instructions regarding War Diaries and Intelligence Summaries are contained in F.S. Regs., Part II. and the Staff Manual respectively. Title pages will be prepared in manuscript.

Hour, Date, Place	Summary of Events and Information	Remarks and references to Appendices
ERQUINGHEM		
Saturday 31st July 1915	All Sections at work as yesterday. Nos. 2 & 3 Sects. started leave at 3.45 p.m.	
Sunday 1st Aug 1915	Sections continued work as yesterday. No 2 Sec. in addition making wooden trough in workshop for use in drainage.	
Monday 2nd Aug. 1915	No. 1 Sec. continue work running & completing dug-outs near Pont du Hem. No 2 Sec. drainage. No. 3 Sec. pumping flooding com. hole at night. No. 4 Sec. continue work on PARK ROW. also work on Ronde Cd & Coy Dug-outs & in workshop	
Tuesday 3rd Aug 1915	Sections continued work as yesterday.	
Wednesday 4th Aug 1915	No. 1 & 2 Sec. Sections continue work as & to be unable to work on Ronde Cd. Have parties on drainage & another working on permanent working party in workshop of M.G. emplacement	
Thursday 5th Aug 1915	Coy Parade at 5.30 p.m. for inspection of arms & ammunition. All Sec. have 6 men at work on Ronde Cd. prepare materials to complete work on Ronde Cd. rest of men engaged in drainage, making ammunition for H.Q. commanding, making around of gate flooring, stopping dug outs light & Sammy Frances Cabaret Rouge. No 4 Sec. in workshop & ready with infantry working on [?] at Box Row.	

Army Form C. 2118.

WAR DIARY
or
INTELLIGENCE SUMMARY.
(Erase heading not required.)

1st Wessex Field Co. R.E.

Instructions regarding War Diaries and Intelligence Summaries are contained in F. S. Regs., Part II. and the Staff Manual respectively. Title pages will be prepared in manuscript.

Hour, Date, Place	Summary of Events and Information	Remarks and references to Appendices
ERQUINGHEM		
Tuesday 10th Aug. 1915	Sections continued work as yesterday. The following Infantry Officers are attached to the Company for R.E. instruction. — Lieut R.S. Tennant, 9th Royal Scots; 2nd Lieut. R.B.S. Reilton 1st R. & S. Highlanders, 2nd Lieut. L.B. Hilke 1st Royal Scots, 2nd Lieut. S. Arnot 2nd Gloucester Regt, 2nd Lieut. A. Pheasey 2nd Gloucester Regt.	
Wednesday 11th Aug 1915	No.1 Section continued revetting tramway communication trench as usual. No.2 Sec. pouring & taking concrete slabs. No.3 Section drainage & dug-outs. No.4 Sec. continued improvement of Pim Pan and party in workshops.	
Thursday 12th Aug 1915	Sections at work as yesterday	
Friday 13th Aug 1915	Do. Do. Do.	
Saturday 14th Aug 1915	Nos. 1, 3 & 4 Sections continued work as before begun. No.2 Section commenced construction of concrete M.G. emplacements in front line. Church Parade at 5.45 p.m.	
Sunday 15th Aug 1915	Sections continued work as before until 1.30 p.m.	
Monday 16th Aug 1915	No.1 Sec. drainage, dug-outs, roofs & flooring. Nos. 2 & 3 Sec. preparing material for concrete M.G. emplacements. 4th Sec. Brigade dug-outs	

Army Form C. 2118.

WAR DIARY
or
INTELLIGENCE SUMMARY.

1st Wessex Field Co. R.E.

(Erase heading not required.)

Instructions regarding War Diaries and Intelligence Summaries are contained in F. S. Regs., Part II and the Staff Manual respectively. Title pages will be prepared in manuscript.

Hour, Date, Place	Summary of Events and Information	Remarks and references to Appendices
ERQUINGHEM.		
Tuesday 17th Aug 1915	Appearing parapet & making fire steps in PRIEZ ROW sent party to Co. workshops. Special respirator & smoke helmet parade. Inspection of arms, iron rations, bayonets &c.	
Wednesday 18th Aug 1915	Sections continued work as yesterday. Tapped off No. 2 & 3 Bourrows. Constructing concrete M.G. emplacement at night.	
	Same as yesterday. Party No. 2 & 3 Bourrows returned to Rept at 3.45 p.m.	
Thursday 19th Aug 1915	No. 1 Sec. drainage by day. Party at night covering stone rush. No. 2 Sec. M.G. emplacement by day. Relaying pipes to reservoir by night. No. 3 Sec. Do. Do. by night in workshops. No. 4 Sec. Revetting tramway communication trench by night. Party in Brigade & Company grounds during day.	
Friday 20th Aug 1915	Sections continued work as yesterday.	
Saturday 21st Aug 1915	Do. Do. Do.	
Sunday 22nd Aug 1915	Do. Do. Do. but returned for dinner at 11.30 am. Kit inspection at 5.15 pm. Church Parade at 6.0 pm.	

Army Form C. 2118.

WAR DIARY
or
INTELLIGENCE SUMMARY.

1st Wessex Field Coy. R.E.

(Erase heading not required.)

Instructions regarding War Diaries and Intelligence Summaries are contained in F.S. Regs., Part II and the Staff Manual respectively. Title pages will be prepared in manuscript.

Hour, Date, Place	Summary of Events and Information	Remarks and references to Appendices
ERQUINGHEM Monday 23rd Aug. 1915	No. 1 Section. Drainage & flooring of trenches. Nos. 2 & 3 Section to concrete M.G. emplacements. No. 4 Section in workshop & out, night party on weekly renders near Convert Farm under Capt. Harvey.	
Tuesday 24th Aug 1915	Sections at work as yesterday. Trench Cath & party on Rendes dug outs.	
Wednesday 25th Aug 1915	Do. Do. Do. Party superintending infantry employed on Brigade dug outs.	
Thursday 26th Aug 1915	Sections employed as before.	
Friday 27th Aug 1915	Party at work on drainage, M.G. emplacements, workshop & fire steps in support line, outside trenches, knocking Rabbit out. Reconned the Gas for Pioneer Regt. & preparing material in workshop. No. 1 Sec. site up trench in advanced trench for covering party.	
Saturday 28th Aug.	Work continued as yesterday.	
Sunday 29th Aug.	Do. Church parade at 5.45 pm.	
Monday 30th Aug 1915	Nos. 2 & 3 Sections engaged trepping track to trench tramway. Other sections at workflow as before.	

WAR DIARY
INTELLIGENCE SUMMARY

(Erase heading not required.)

Army Form C. 2118.

1st Sussex Field Co. R.E.

Instructions regarding War Diaries and Intelligence Summaries are contained in F. S. Regs., Part II and the Staff Manual respectively. Title pages will be prepared in manuscript.

Hour, Date, Place	Summary of Events and Information	Remarks and references to Appendices
ERQUINGHEM. Tuesday 31st Aug 15	Ock from No 1 Section in morning shewing that Billets from No 2 & 3 Section on reconnaissance of support line. Party from No 2 Sec. at work on support line. At night each section provided NCOs & men for work on [illegible] from. He keeps and until 3 a.m. the new trench of railway embankment sad. [illegible] from sunken farm to the front line is in use now.	
Wednesday 1st Sept 15	Sections at work as yesterday. Ditto. [illegible] new trench at railway embankment. Party at night.	
Thursday 2nd Sept 15	Sections continued work on new [illegible]. NCO employment on work as yesterday and on [illegible] trenches.	
Friday 3rd Sept 15	[illegible]	
Saturday 4th Sept 15	No 2 Sec. improving [illegible] & widening of support trenches in advance of [illegible] line [illegible]. No 3 Sec. continuing [illegible] [illegible] in support line & [illegible]. Sniping posts at night in [illegible] trenches [illegible] shelters [illegible] to [illegible] in [illegible].	

WAR DIARY or INTELLIGENCE SUMMARY

Army Form C. 2118.

1st Wessex Field Co. R.E.

Hour, Date, Place	Summary of Events and Information	Remarks and references to Appendices

ERQUINGHEM
Sunday 5th Sept/15

Parties of Nos 1 & 2 Sections as work on commenced dugouts on concrete emplacement for field gun in front line and preparing material. Rest of Nos 1 Sec. on standdown.
No. 3 Sec. on emplacement in mountain gun in front line.
No 4 Sec. on work on support line & in workshops as before.

Monday 6th Sept 1915

Nos 1 & 2 Sections continue work on field gun emplacement & concrete bunker on revetting trenches on CRAY ROW and at BURNT FARM. No 3 Section on French M.G. emplacements & repairing material. No 4 Section in workshops & providing reliefs for standing dug-outs & other work.

Tuesday 7th Sept 1915

Sections as employed as yesterday.

Wednesday 8th Sept.

No. 1 Sec. on drainage near COLLEGE GREEN and in SHAFTESBURY AVENUE
No 2 Sec. on rear gun position in front line & preparing material
No 3 Sec. M.G. Emplacements as before.
No 4 Sec. Revetting parapet & revetting firing steps on support line.

Thursday 9th Sept.

Sections employed as yesterday.

Army Form C. 2118.

WAR DIARY

INTELLIGENCE SUMMARY.

(Erase heading not required.)

1/1st Sussex Field Co. R.E.

Instructions regarding War Diaries and Intelligence Summaries are contained in F. S. Regs., Part II. and the Staff Manual respectively. Title pages will be prepared in manuscript.

Hour, Date, Place	Summary of Events and Information	Remarks and references to Appendices
ERQUINGHEM.		
1st Sept 1915	Sections carried work as before. Capt. Harris made tour of the work with Major Boston of the 103rd Field Co. R.E. who was to take over section on explaining all work at present in hand.	
2nd Sept 1915	Major Boston checked R.E. on knowledge of sections and of sections working in trenches.	
3rd Sept 1915	[illegible handwritten entry]	

Army Form C. 2118.

WAR DIARY
or
INTELLIGENCE SUMMARY.

(1st Wessex Field Co. R.E.)

(Erase heading not required.)

Instructions regarding War Diaries and Intelligence Summaries are contained in F. S. Regs., Part II. and the Staff Manual respectively. Title pages will be prepared in manuscript.

Hour, Date, Place	Summary of Events and Information	Remarks and references to Appendices
BLEUTOUR. 16th Sept 1915.	Company paraded in full marching order at 6.30 p.m. & marched via CROIX DU BAC, ESTAIRES, NEUF BERQUIN to BLEUTOUR near MERRIS where the men billeted in a farm. Although a night march of about 14 miles, moral, discipline and morale of men exceedingly good & there were no stragglers.	
17th Sept 1915	Company rested for the day as some billets had fallen short from others.	
18th Sept 1915	Sappers did a gun platform, drill & took a short route march.	
	Green recommenced road from BLEUTOUR to THIENNES.	
19th Sept 1915	Company left farm at BLEUTOUR at 4.0 p.m. via VIEUX BERQUIN, CARESCURE, FORÊT DE NIEPPE & TANNAY to THIENNES reaching the latter place at 10.0 p.m. Here the Coy. entrained.	
THIENNES 20th Sept 1915	Train left THIENNES at 2.28 a.m. & travelled via ABBEVILLE and AMIENS to GUILLAUCOURT where we arrived at 11.45 a.m. The company detrained immediately after arrival & afterwards marched via BOISTONVILLERS, CERISY and MORCOURT to its destination at MERICOURT. Here the men were billeted in some old huts near the Square in the village.	
MERICOURT 21st Sept 1915	Sappers cleaned up & rearranged billets which had recently been occupied by French troops & collected furniture & little articles in order that wagons might be used for hauling R.E. material.	

Army Form C. 2118.

WAR DIARY
or
INTELLIGENCE SUMMARY.

1st Sussex Field Co. R.E.

(Erase heading not required.)

Instructions regarding War Diaries and Intelligence Summaries are contained in F. S. Regs., Part II. and the Staff Manual respectively. Title pages will be prepared in manuscript.

Hour, Date, Place	Summary of Events and Information	Remarks and references to Appendices
MERCOURT		
22nd Sept 1915	Party of Sappers prepared explosion of land engines to our 1st Delivered bombs thrown. Rest of Company engaged making Lewisson trestles & carry bodies for use in front line.	
23rd Sept 1915	Sappers continued work on yesterday. Party of sappers taking flare lights at MERCOURT. Used have trestle to saw with where lathes path. Set work on circular saw.	
24th Sept 1915	Do Do Do	
25th Sept 1915	Do Do Do. No 2 Section engaged making beams for road. Bearers of bridges to carry heavy ones over new bridge.	
26th Sept 1915	Sappers continued similar work to previous day.	
27th Sept 1915	No 1 Section leave for work at ECLUSIER. Sappers of No 2, 3 & 4 Section continue work as yesterday.	
28th Sept 1915	No 2 Section start construction of trestle bridge across the canal near cappy. Other sappers continue work as before.	

(73989) W4141—463. 400,000. 9/14. H.&J.Ltd. Forms/C. 2118/10.

Army Form C. 2118.

WAR DIARY

Stevens Lt. Co. R.E.

INTELLIGENCE SUMMARY.

(Erase heading not required.)

Instructions regarding War Diaries and Intelligence Summaries are contained in F. S. Regs., Part II. and the Staff Manual respectively. Title pages will be prepared in manuscript.

Hour, Date, Place	Summary of Events and Information	Remarks and references to Appendices
MERICOURT. 29th Sept 1915	Nos. 1 & 4 Section continue making trestles & ladders, Bench standards & cutting pickets for revetting purposes. No. 2 Section on trestle bridge near CHIPPY. No. 3 Section find party for circular saw, loading heavy logs on trestle wagon & work on Font Shelters.	
30th Sept 1915	Nos. 1 & 4 Behind under 2/Lieut Jones & Lloyd move to CHUIGNOLLES for work in the front line. Nos. 2 & 3 Sections continue work as yesterday.	R.N. Quittin Major R.E. O/C 1st W. & M. Cy.

WAR DIARY

1st Wessex Field Co. R.E.

Army Form C. 2118.

INTELLIGENCE SUMMARY.

(Erase heading not required.)

Hour, Date, Place	Summary of Events and Information	Remarks and references to Appendices
MERICOURT-S-SOMME		
1st October 1915	Nos. 1 & 2 Sections at CHUIGNOLLES taken over work in front line from 2nd Wessex Fd. Co. No. 2 Section at work on bridge across canal near CAPPY. No. 3 Section sent parties for work on new bench & making mushroom trestles & trench platforms.	
2nd October 1915	Sappers continued work as yesterday.	
3rd " "	No. 2 Section from Becourt busy in canal, other sections continued work as before.	
4th October 1915	No. 2 Section return to work on bridge near CAPPY. No. 2 R.E. & Infy. Party went with Lieut. Peat & is attached to Capt. R.E. Indian Sapper (O.M. Volunteered to assist while on unexpected arrival in new war. Sections continued work already in hand.	
5th October 1915	No. 2 & 3 Sections leave for Jeanean billets at BUIRONNE les BRAY & take over front line work of No. 1/4 Wessex Fd Co. at CHUIGNOLLES. Lieut. Richmond of 108th Fd. Co. R.E. is attached to No. 3 Section to gain experience of front line work.	
6th " "	Lieut. L. Mercer of 7th Royal Scots is attached to Co. for instruction. No Company takes over R.E. Park CHUIGNOLLES for ...	

Army Form C. 2118.

WAR DIARY
or
INTELLIGENCE SUMMARY.
(Erase heading not required.)

1st Wessex Ft. Co. R.E.

Instructions regarding War Diaries and Intelligence Summaries are contained in F. S. Regs., Part II. and the Staff Manual respectively. Title pages will be prepared in manuscript.

Hour, Date, Place	Summary of Events and Information	Remarks and references to Appendices
MERICOURT-S-SOMME. 7th October 1915.	No. 1 Section forging new billets at CHUIGNOLLES. No. 2 Sec. party digging dug out at Foraine le Crecy. Remainder of Section digging retrenchment behind PRIAH with infantry. No. 3 Section on retrenchment for two days ahead JERMNY with infantry. No. 4 Section trenches & shower positions round.	
8th October 1915.	No. 1 Section on new Brigade shelters at FONTAINE LES CAPPY. No. 2, 3 & 4 Sections continued work as yesterday.	
9th October 1915.	Sappers continue work as above. Company HQrs. removed from MERICOURT-SUR-SOMME to CHUIGNOLLES.	
CHUIGNOLLES 10th October 1915.	Nos. 2 & 3 Sections continue night work in front line with infantry parties. No. 1 & 4 Sections rest.	
11th October 1915.	No. 1 Section continue work on Brigade shelters at FONTAINE LES CAPPY. Nos. 2 & 3 Section night work in front line. No. 4 Section making knifewood hurdles & other shelter material. Party in carriage of same at CHUIGNES.	
12th October 1915.	Nos. 1 & 4 Sections relieve Nos. 2 & 3 Sections at FONTAINE LES CAPPY and take over work on front line. Nos. 2 & 3 Sections return to billets at	

WAR DIARY
or
INTELLIGENCE SUMMARY.

(Erase heading not required.)

Army Form C. 2118.

1st Bn/de 5th Co. R.E.

Instructions regarding War Diaries and Intelligence Summaries are contained in F. S. Regs., Part II and the Staff Manual respectively. Title pages will be prepared in manuscript.

Hour, Date, Place	Summary of Events and Information	Remarks and references to Appendices
CHUIGNOLLES 13th Oct 1918	CHUIGNOLLES. Whole Company billeted at FROYART. Recd. copy of O.O. 5th Co. R.E. in which we are detailed to proceed forward in front the advancing 2nd Regiment and return to the Company.	
H.Q. Billets 9.15	No. 1 & 2 Sections reported sick next morning when a retirement from FROYART and VIBRAY road was declared to be advisable. No. 2 Sec. on Brigade Hd Qrs at FONTAINE-LES-CAPPY. No. 3 Sec. making Rubble Road for transport.	
Recce party 9.15	An or Section recce made to ± 3 See m/vement up to Ridge near CAPPY & on Brigade dugouts at FONTAINE from a ridge in front the Panzers.	
At Brickworks 9.15	All Sections again now in Reserve. R.E.5 Section work on main traffic road from line. Bn 1 Sec making road in Ridge in Brigade dug outs.	
W.G. Bricks 9.15	Wireless Wallet + under telephone line to 5 Sub. between Brick Route at CHUIGNOLLES. No. 1 & 2 Sections continued to get the	

Army Form C. 2118.

WAR DIARY
of 1st Wessex Field Co. R.E.

INTELLIGENCE SUMMARY.
(Erase heading not required.)

Instructions regarding War Diaries and Intelligence Summaries are contained in F. S. Regs., Part II. and the Staff Manual respectively. Title pages will be prepared in manuscript.

Hour, Date, Place	Summary of Events and Information	Remarks and references to Appendices
CHUIGNOLLES. 18th October 1915	Company Hd. Qrs. move to MERICOURT-SUR-SOMME with Nos. 2 & 3 Sections and take over work in 2nd line from 108th Co. R.E. No.1 Sec. remained to MERICOURT from FONTAINE-LES-CAPPY. No.4 Sec. continue work in front line at night.	
MERICOURT 19th October 1915	No.1 Sec. take over repair of roads. No.2 Section with company carpenter commence construction of new workshops. No.3 Section superintend infantry parties on improvement of 2nd line between CHUIGNOLLES and PROYART. No.4 Sec. under Lieut Shepherd leave FONTAINE-LES-CAPPY for CAPPY where they take over work in redoubts COY AU VERGER, OLYMPE, BOIS CARRÉ and FROISSY from 108th Coy R.E.	
20th October 1915	Sections continue work as yesterday. Do.	
21st October 1915	Do. Do.	
22nd October 1915	Sappers check tool carts & pontoon superstructure, wash down No. Qrs. & Section wagons & load pontoon & trestle wagons. No.4 Section leave CAPPY and return to MERICOURT	
23rd October 1915	No.1 Section on bridge near CAPPY. Remainder of sappers continue bracketwork trestles & trench footboards in wood	

WAR DIARY or INTELLIGENCE SUMMARY.

Army Form C. 2118.

(Erase heading not required.)

1st Section 1st E. R. E.

Hour, Date, Place	Summary of Events and Information	Remarks and references to Appendices
MERICOURT 24th October 1915	Company paraded at 9 a.m. and marched to BOVES via MORCOURT, WARFUSEE-ABANCOURT, & VILLERS-BRETONNEUX. Maj. Gen. failed to inspect the Company en route & congratulated the O.C. & the men on their appearance & on the manner in which the company & general moved interested. The Coy. bivouacked for the night at BOVES. (Raining)	
BOVES 25th October 1915	The Coy. left BOVES at 10.30 a.m. & continued the march via St. FUSCIEN, DURY, SALEUX & PISSY to SEUX arriving there at 5.30 p.m. Billets in barns. Billets not arranged for, & many men lay out but in spite of this the officers & billets found for men extremely well.	
SEUX 26th October 1915	The Coy. paraded at 8.15 a.m. & continued march via PISSY, FREMONT and FRICAMPS to HERMAVILLY from THIEULLOY-L'ABBAYE where the Coy. arrived at 10 p.m. Baggage wagons completely littered on the road, losing two large guns & all the Police were disabled. Wine & canned goods.	
HERMAVILLY 27th October 1915	Baggage parade for kits & drill instruction & afternoon work when all company left. By order of G.O.C. 82nd Brigade a Coys. & a.m. men parade on a fatigue at HERMAVILLY under W.O. S. or GUDRY. Billets examined passed & clean parades.	

WAR DIARY

1st Wessex Fd. Co. R.E.

INTELLIGENCE SUMMARY.

(Erase heading not required.)

Army Form C. 2118.

Hour, Date, Place	Summary of Events and Information	Remarks and references to Appendices
HERMILLY 28th October 1915	Sappers – rifle & drill instruction Drivers – exercise horses & clean harness	
29th October 1915	As yesterday	
30th " "	Sappers – 1 hour rifle & drill instruction " 2 hours instruction in R.E. work under Section Officers Drivers – as before.	
31st October 1915	Sappers – 1 hour rifle & drill instruction " 2 hours horse parade. Drivers – exercise horses & continue ploughing of Farmers	

R.R. Buckney Major
O/C 1st Wx Field Coy R.E.

CONFIDENTIAL.

WAR DIARY

OF

1ST WESSEX FIELD COMPANY R.E. (T.F.)

27TH DIVISION

Vol V

From 1st Nov 1915 To 30th November 1915

Army Form C. 2118.

WAR DIARY
or
INTELLIGENCE SUMMARY.

1st/1st Wessex Field Co. R.E.
2nd Wessex Field Co. R.E.

(Erase heading not required.)

Instructions regarding War Diaries and Intelligence Summaries are contained in F.S. Regs., Part II. and the Staff Manual respectively. Title pages will be prepared in manuscript.

Hour, Date, Place	Summary of Events and Information	Remarks and references to Appendices
HERMILLY		
1st November 1915	Sappers :- 1 hour rifle & drill instruction. Instruction in R.E. work } under Section Officers. in afternoon 2 hour route march. Drivers :- Exercise horses & clean harness.	
2nd November 1915	As yesterday.	
3rd " "	do. Inspection of horses & harness by O.C.	
4th " "	do. Inspection of arms, equipment, ammunition, smoke helmets, &c.	
5th " "	Sappers continue instruction as on 1st. do. do. do. Bridging equipment checked & return of deficiencies & unserviceable stores made. Section pool cart saddlery checked.	
6th " "	Sappers :- rifle & drill instruction & instruction in R.E. work under Section Officers. Drivers :- Exercise horses, clean harness &c.	
7th " "	do. do. new draft of six men arrive from Base.	

WAR DIARY

INTELLIGENCE SUMMARY.

Army Form C. 2118.

of 1st Sussex Field Co. R.E.

Instructions regarding War Diaries and Intelligence Summaries are contained in F.S. Regs., Part II and the Staff Manual respectively. Title pages will be prepared in manuscript.

(Erase heading not required.)

Hour, Date, Place	Summary of Events and Information	Remarks and references to Appendices
HERMILLY 8th November 1915	Sappers :- 1 hours rifle & drill instruction. Inspection of clothing, boots &c. Inspection of new shafts by O.C. 1 hours instruction in engineering by Senior Officer.	
	Drivers :- exercise, horses & routine cleaning of lines.	
9th November 1915	Sappers continue instruction as yesterday.	
10h "	Do.	
11h " "	Do.	
	Horses are returned to depot at POPERINGHE and we obtain in exchange, in accordance with new scheme, others.	
12h " "	Sappers continue instruction as before. Drivers - new animals arriving & being exercised.	
13h " "	Do yesterday	
14h " "	"	
15h " "	Sappers continue instruction in drill & R.E. work. New horsed R.E. wagons drawn in accordance with new establishment.	

Army Form C. 2118.

WAR DIARY
1st Essex Field Co. R.E.
INTELLIGENCE SUMMARY.
(Erase heading not required.)

Instructions regarding War Diaries and Intelligence Summaries are contained in F.S. Regs., Part II and the Staff Manual respectively. Title pages will be prepared in manuscript.

Hour, Date, Place	Summary of Events and Information	Remarks and references to Appendices
HERMILLY 15th Nov 1915	Sappers :- 1 Hour's rifle & drill instruction. 2" instruction in engineering } by Section Officers Inspection of arms. Drivers :- exercise horses & mules & continue cleaning harness which was issued in very bad condition.	
16th Nov 1915	As yesterday. Sappers also practice packing new vehicles & Drivers harnessing & exercising new mule teams.	
17th Nov 1915	Drill & R.E. instruction continued as yesterday. Church Parade at 3.30 pm followed by Holy Communion.	
18th Nov 1915	Section Officers continue instruction of Sappers in R.E. work. Inspection of horses, draught mules & harness by O.C.	
19th Nov 1915	1 Hour's rifle & drill instruction. 2 Hours route march. Do. Do. Sappers practice packing	
20th Nov 1915	Technical stores & loading vehicles.	

WAR DIARY
or
INTELLIGENCE SUMMARY.

(Erase heading not required.)

Army Form C. 2118.

1st Sussex Field Co. R.E.

Instructions regarding War Diaries and Intelligence Summaries are contained in F.S. Regs., Part II. and the Staff Manual respectively. Title pages will be prepared in manuscript.

Hour, Date, Place.	Summary of Events and Information	Remarks and references to Appendices
HERMIVAL 21st November 1915	Rifle & drill instruction as before. No. 1 & 2 Sections practice pontoon drill in morning. No. 3 & 4 Sections in afternoon.	
22nd Nov. 1915	Company leave HERMIVAL at 10.30 a.m. and march via ST. PIERRE, BOURGINVILLE, FROICOURT & BRIQUEMESNIL to new billets at SAISSEVAL arriving at 2.30 p.m.	
SAISSEVAL 23rd Nov. 1915	Sections continue tools & drill instruction and R.E. work. In afternoon 1 hour's physical drill.	
24th Nov. 1915	Training work as yesterday. Route march in afternoon.	
25th Nov. 1915	As yesterday	
26th Nov. 1915	Do. Do.	
27th Nov 1915	Do. Do. 2 Officers are detailed to meet Drivers of horse lines. 6 men and 31 drivers short of new establishment. Have difficulty in getting new draft.	
28th Nov. 1915	Company attend Church Parade at ROUELLES.	

Army Form C. 2118.

WAR DIARY
of 1st Wessex Field Co. R.E.
~~INTELLIGENCE SUMMARY.~~
(Erase heading not required.)

Instructions regarding War Diaries and Intelligence Summaries are contained in F.S. Regs., Part II. and the Staff Manual respectively. Title pages will be prepared in manuscript.

Hour, Date, Place	Summary of Events and Information	Remarks and references to Appendices
SAISSEVAL 29th November 1915.	Sappers continue instruction under Section Officers. Drivers exercise horses & mules & continue cleaning harness.	
30th Nov. 1915.	50 Sappers detailed for work at BOVELLES. Remainder continue instruction as before.	

R.D. Buchanan
Major
O/C 1st Wessex Field Coy R.E.

CONFIDENTIAL

WAR DIARY

OF

1ST WESSEX FIELD COY R.E. (T.F.) - 27TH DIV

Vol VI

From 1st Dec 1915 to 31st Dec 1915

Army Form C. 2118.

WAR DIARY
of
1st Wessex Field Co. R.E.
INTELLIGENCE SUMMARY.
(Erase heading not required.)

Instructions regarding War Diaries and Intelligence Summaries are contained in F.S. Regs., Part II and the Staff Manual respectively. Title pages will be prepared in manuscript.

Hour, Date, Place	Summary of Events and Information	Remarks and references to Appendices
SAISSEVAL 1st December 1915.	Sappers – Rifle & drill instruction under Section Officers. Route march in afternoon. Drivers – Exercise horses & mules & clean harness.	
2nd Dec. 1915	Sappers – Rifle drill & engineering instruction under Section Officers. Drivers – As before.	
3rd Dec. 1915	Do. Do. Do.	
4 Dec. 1915	Pontooning practice on the canal at PICQUIGNY.	
5 " "	Company attends Church Parade at BOVELLES.	
6 " "	No. Company leaves SAISSEVAL at 11.0 a.m. & marches via BOVELLES & GUIGNEMICOURT to CLAIRY arriving here at 1.30 p.m. Billeted for night.	
CLAIRY 7/h " "	Whole Company including fld. Qr. sergeant, leave CLAIRY at 11.0 a.m. & march with 17½ Fld. Co. R.E. to LONGUEAU Station where they entrained in afternoon. Capt. S. Harvey in charge. Train left LONGUEAU at 7.25 p.m. for MARSEILLES.	

WAR DIARY
INTELLIGENCE SUMMARY
(Erase heading not required.)

Army Form C. 2118.

1/1st Sussex Field Co. R.E.

Hour, Date, Place	Summary of Events and Information	Remarks and references to Appendices
CLARY 7th Decr 1915 (cont.)	Remainder of Company leave CLARY at 2.0 p.m. & march with 2nd Sussex Field Co. R.E. & Infantry details to LONGUEAU Station where they entrained for MARSEILLES. Train left at 9.15 p.m.	
8th Decr 1915	Travelling all day & all night.	
9th " "	Arrived MARSEILLES about 6.0 a.m. O.C. detrained at PRSVC Station. Company under 2nd in Exposition Ground. Was Kind Point. My Coy stopped Company remained at the Prago Station. Arrived tents camping ground arriving there about 9.30 a.m.	
MARSEILLES 10th " "	Spent part of day arranging & supervision of new tents - march and of various field tents & various amounts	
11th " "	No Company duties moreover camp fatigues + R.E. Parades + Games + Inspections & arrangements	
12th " "	Church Parade at 9.15 a.m. Guard mount never August + H.P. Where found	

Army Form C. 2118.

WAR DIARY
1st Essex Field Co. R.E.
INTELLIGENCE SUMMARY.
(Erase heading not required.)

Instructions regarding War Diaries and Intelligence Summaries are contained in F.S. Regs., Part II. and the Staff Manual respectively. Title pages will be prepared in manuscript.

Hour, Date, Place	Summary of Events and Information	Remarks and references to Appendices
MARSEILLES 13th December 1915	180 men attend Baths. Orders received at 12 noon for Company to move to BORELY PARC. Company left EXPOSITION Grounds at 2.15 p.m. & arrived at new camping ground at 4.45 p.m. where all men were accommodated under canvas.	
BORELY PARC MARSEILLES. 14th December 1915 to 31st December 1915	The Company remained in Camp at BORELY PARC throughout this period. Camp guards, fatigues & other duties were found & a good deal of drainage work carried out. Sappers were also given stepped field rifle & engineering instruction & generally a short route march every day.	
Xmas Day	The Company attended Church Parade at 9.0 a.m. Peace and quiet reigned during the afternoon & in the evening a Xmas Dinner was provided after which a smoking concert was held. All had a thoroughly enjoyable day. The men's behaviour was excellent.	

R.B. Dutton Major R.E.

www.ingramcontent.com/pod-product-compliance
Lightning Source LLC
Chambersburg PA
CBHW081453160426
43193CB00013B/2459